To my beloved parents
Thank you for raising me and showing me how to love the Lord and serve others with a joyful heart
And to Maverick for bringing smiles to so many people's faces

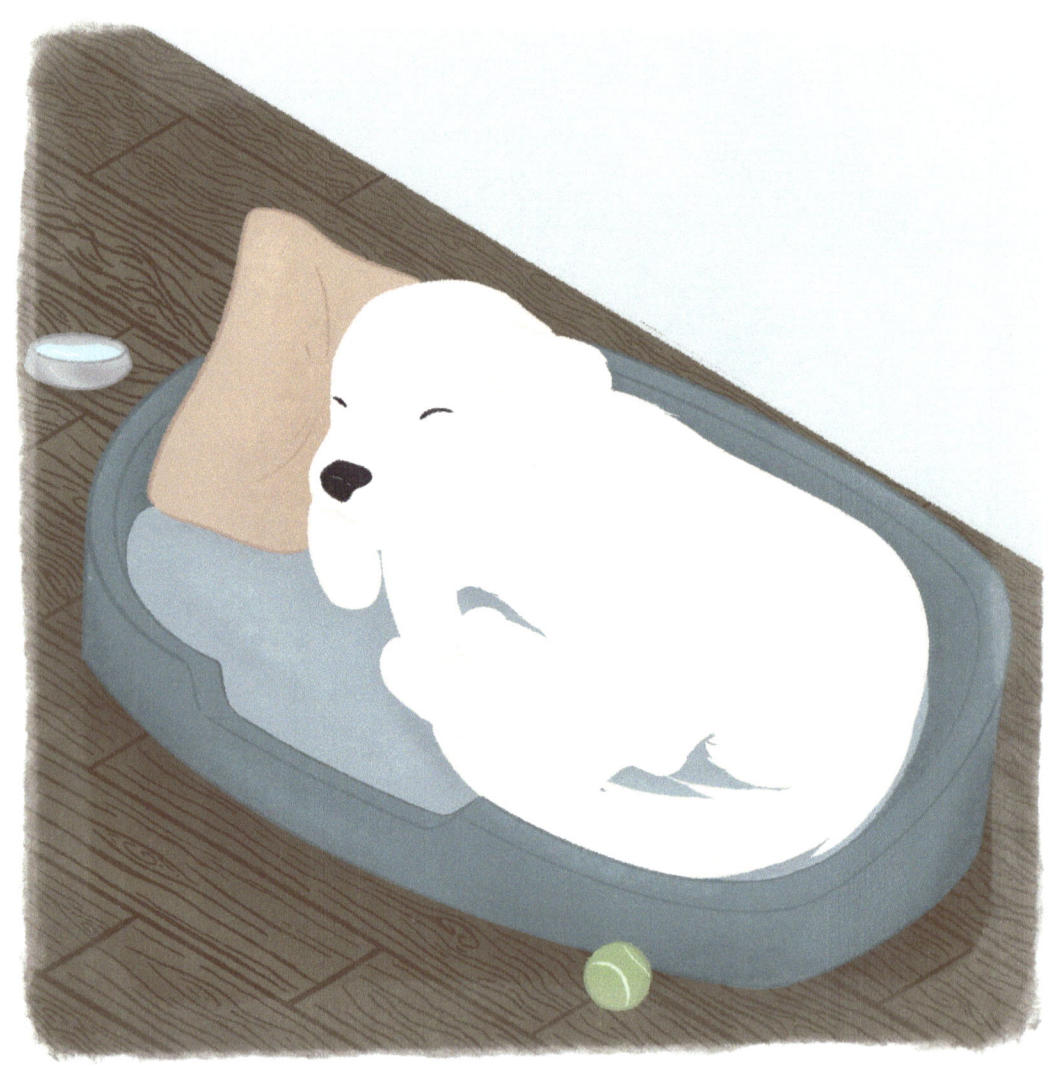

It was a peaceful morning and Maverick was sound asleep when his big brother Nash came over to wake him up.

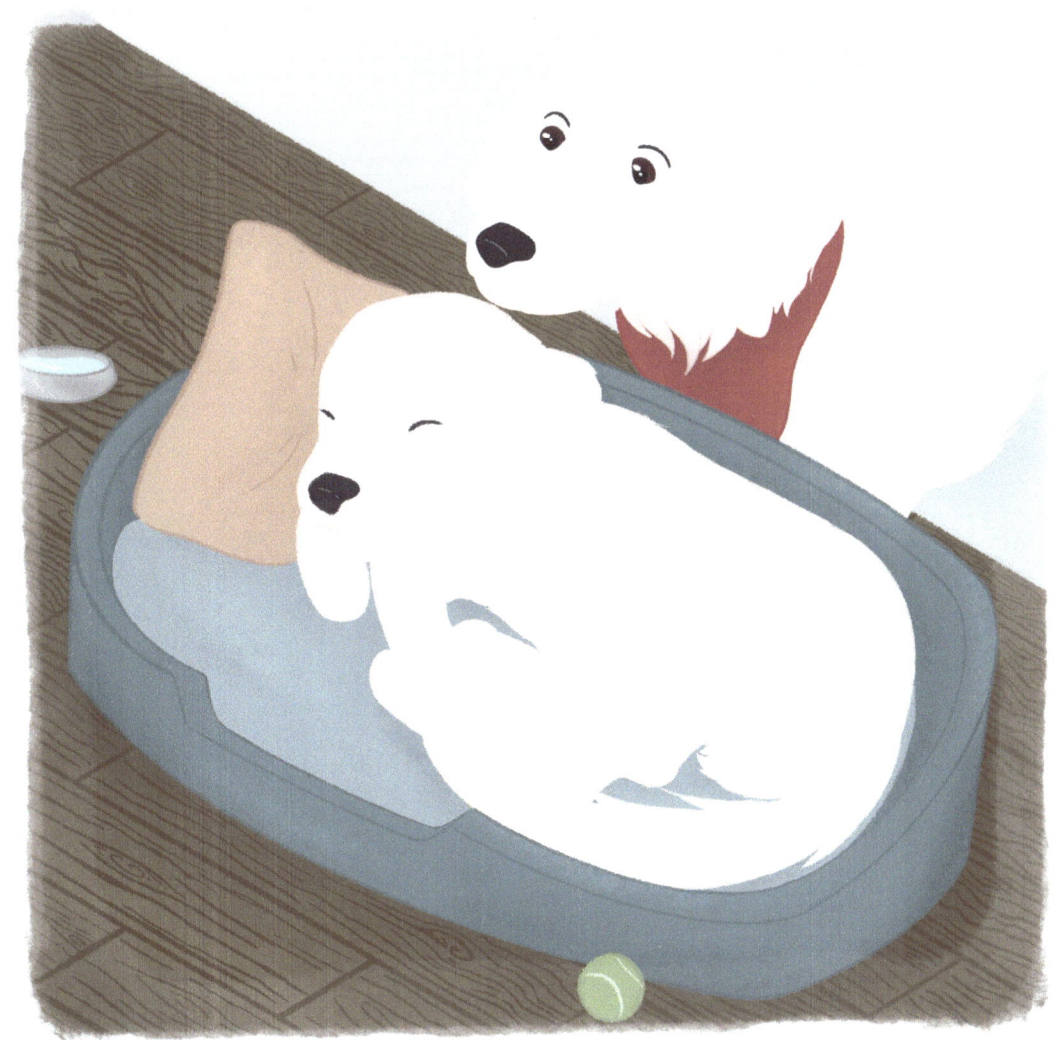

"Maverick. Little brother." Nash nudged Maverick. "It's time to wake up."

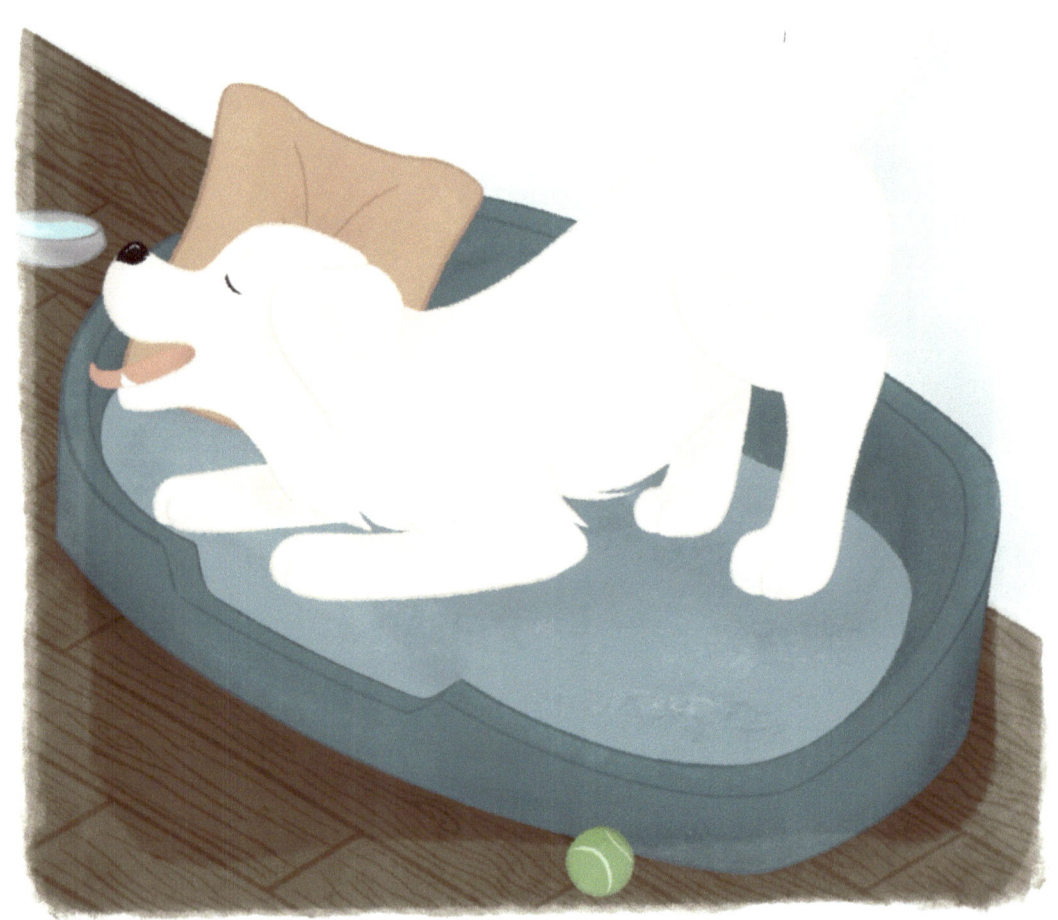

"Where are we going big brother?" Maverick asked as he yawned and stretched his legs.

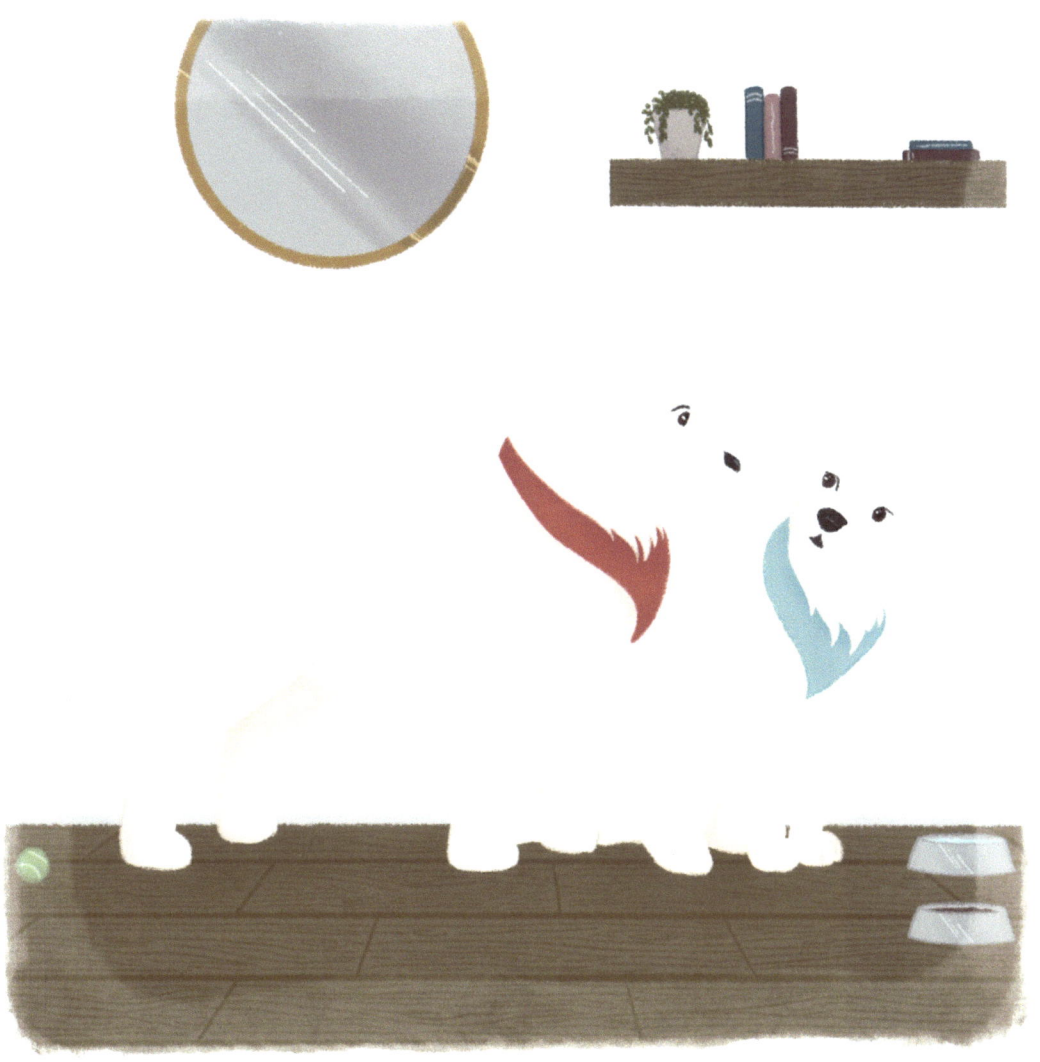

"We're going to go serve." Nash said. Maverick looked at Nash with a quizzical brow. "Serve? What does that mean?"

"We're going to give our time by helping others."
Nash said as he ate his breakfast.

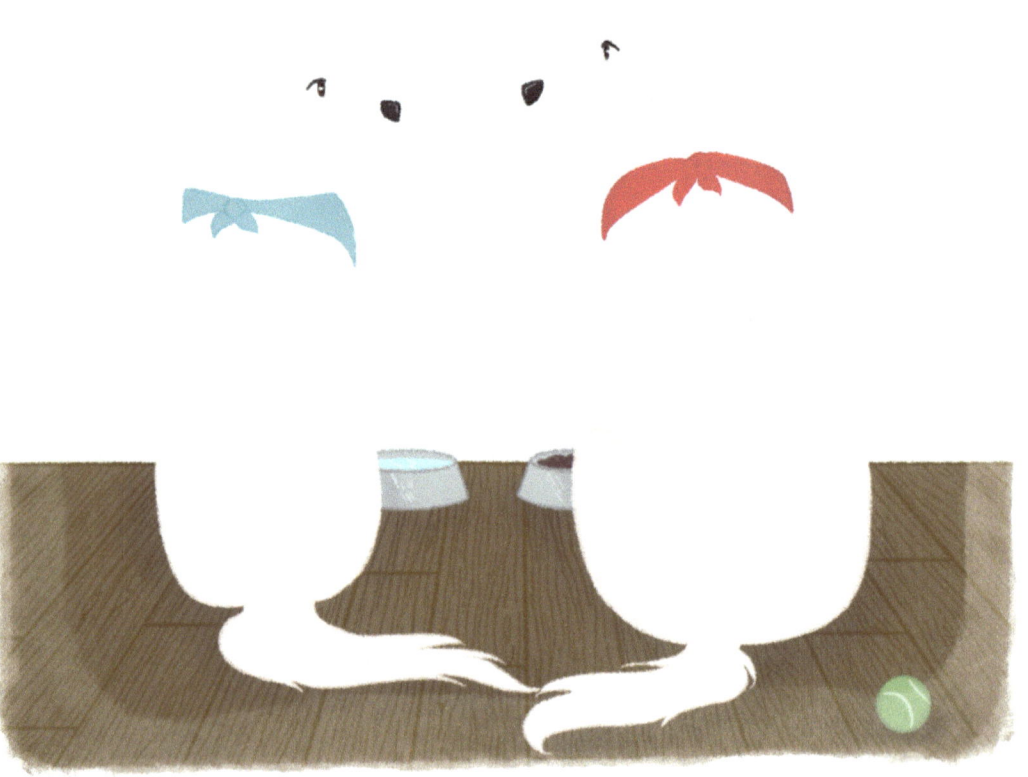

"But why? It's so early in the morning!" Maverick groaned.
"Because, it's the right thing to do." Nash chuckled. "Now eat your breakfast."

After breakfast, Maverick and Nash hopped in their truck to go to the serve event.

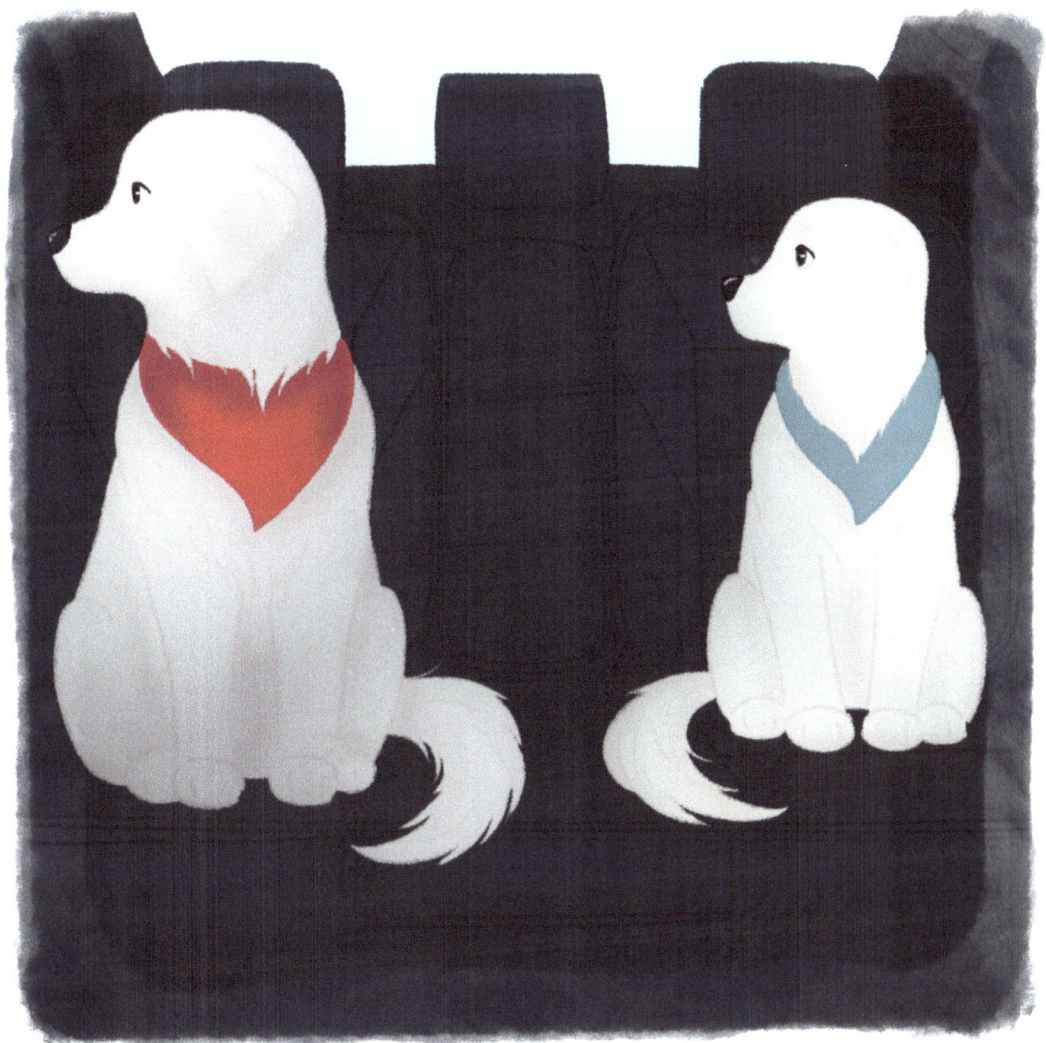

When they were on their way, Maverick turned to Nash and asked him, "How exactly are we going to serve others?"

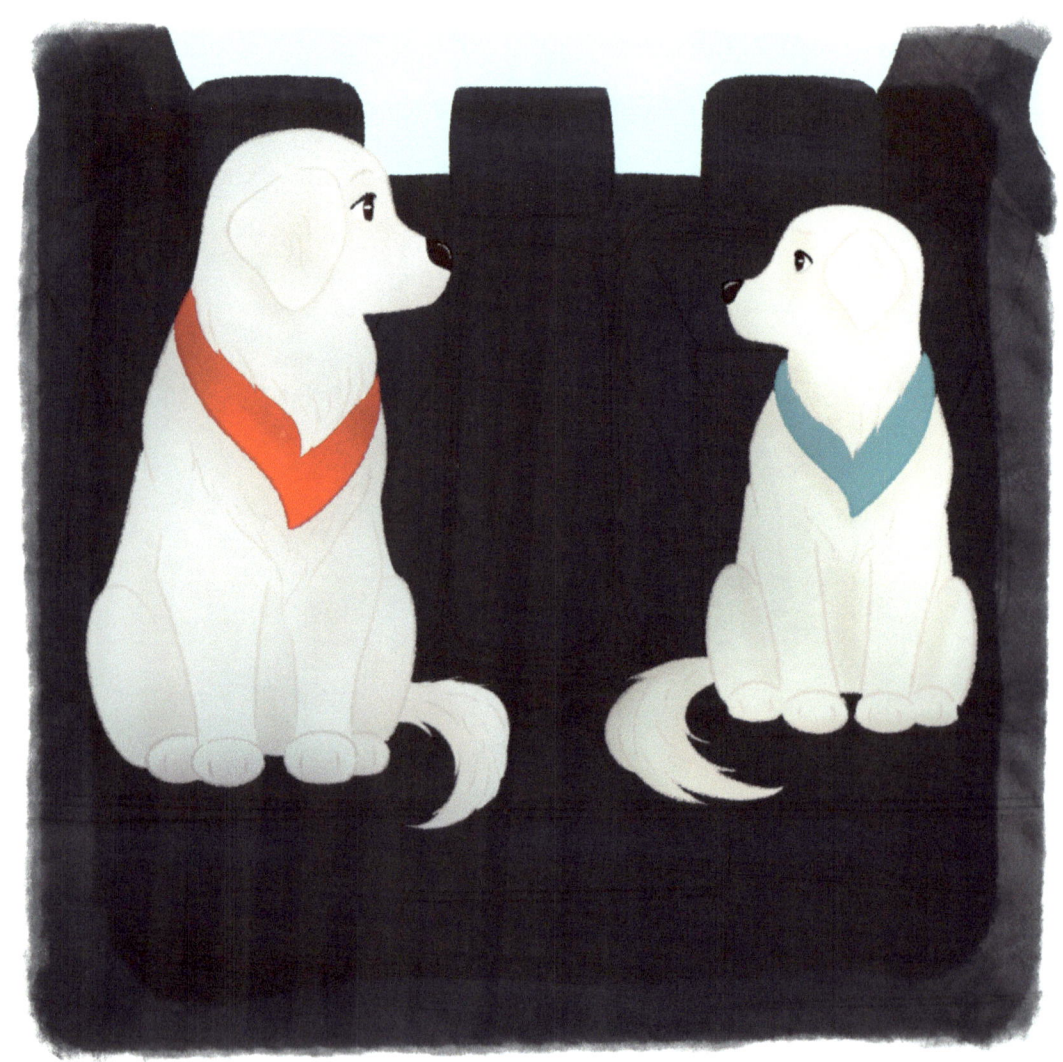

Nash turned to look at Maverick, "Well, today we are going to visit children in the hospital."

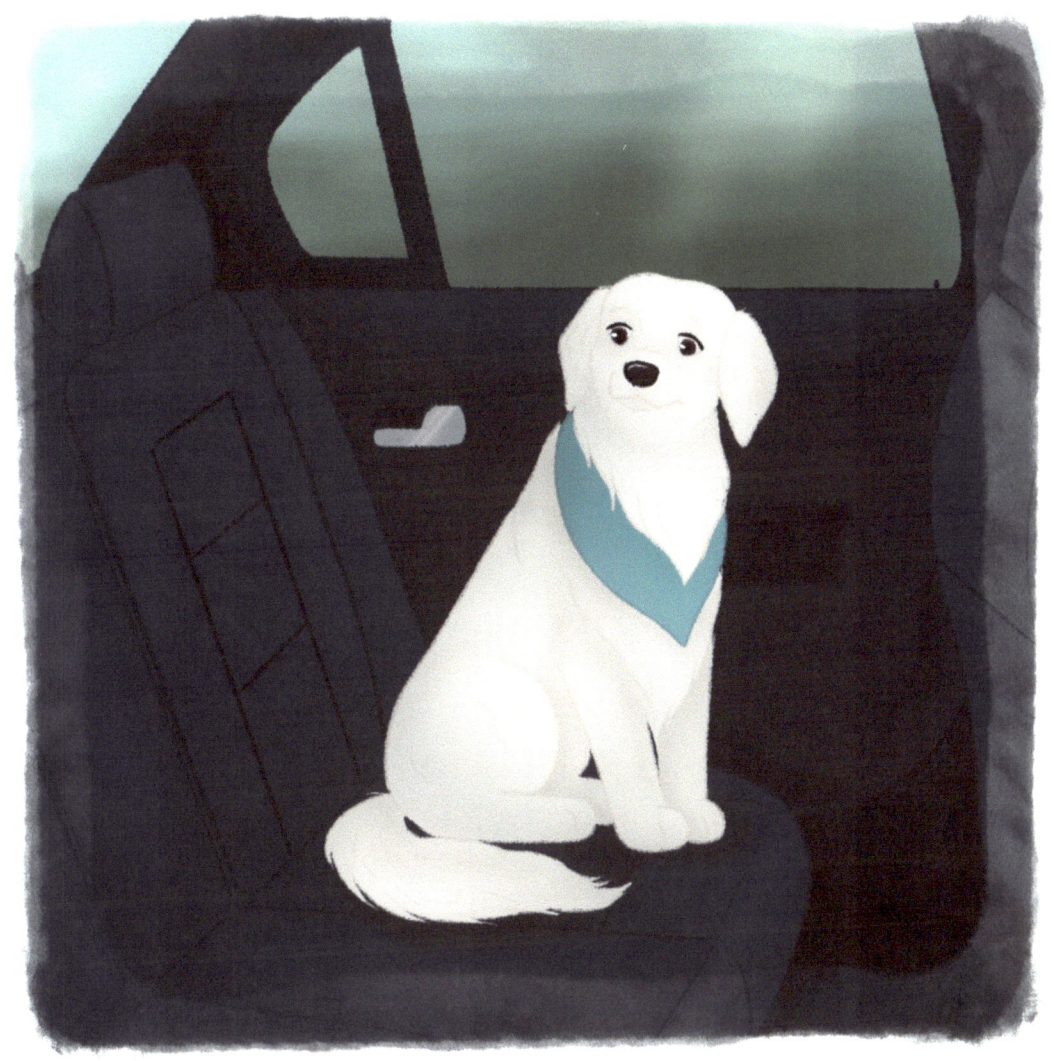

"In the hospital?" Maverick questioned with concern.

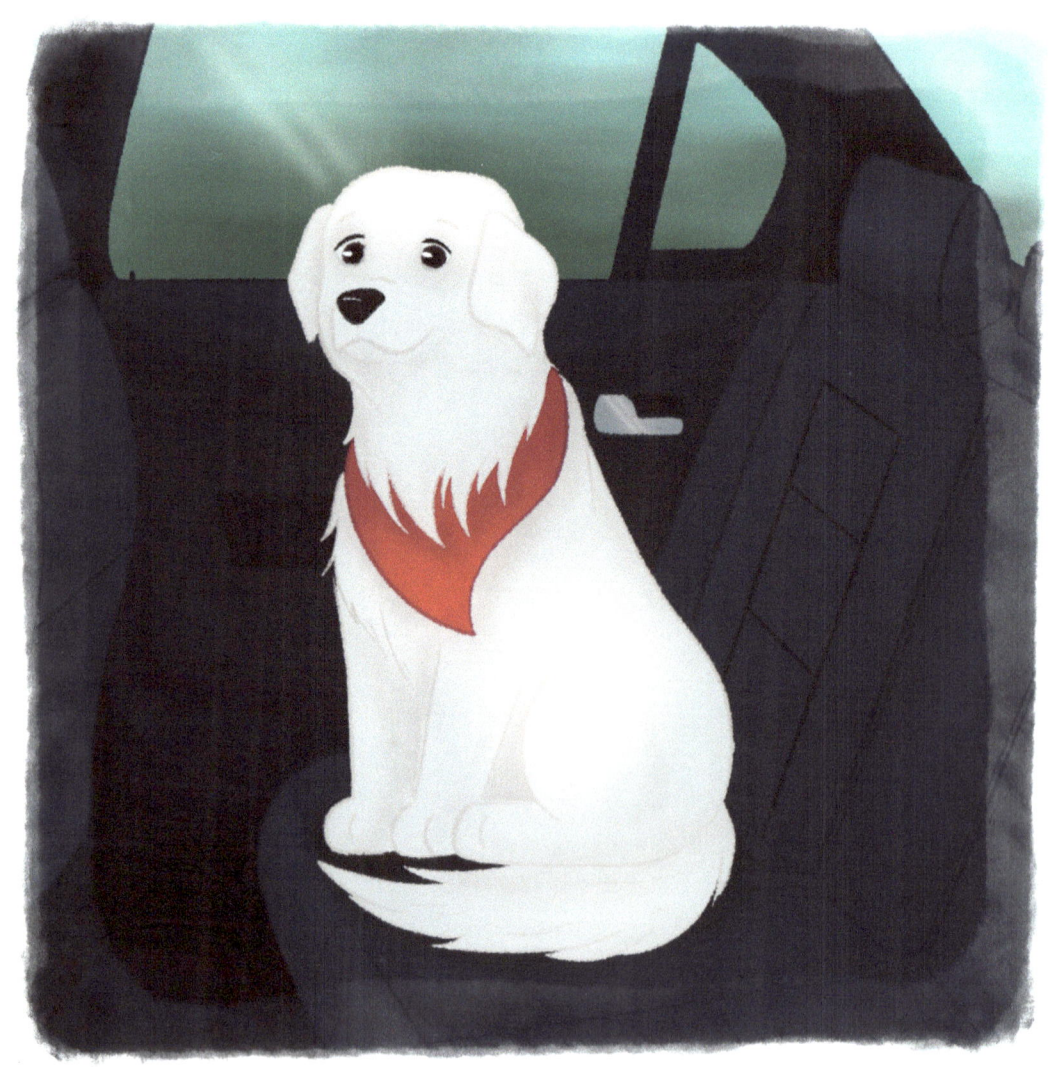

"Yes." Nash said with a smile. "You see, some people have to stay in the hospital to get better and being in the hospital can make them sad."

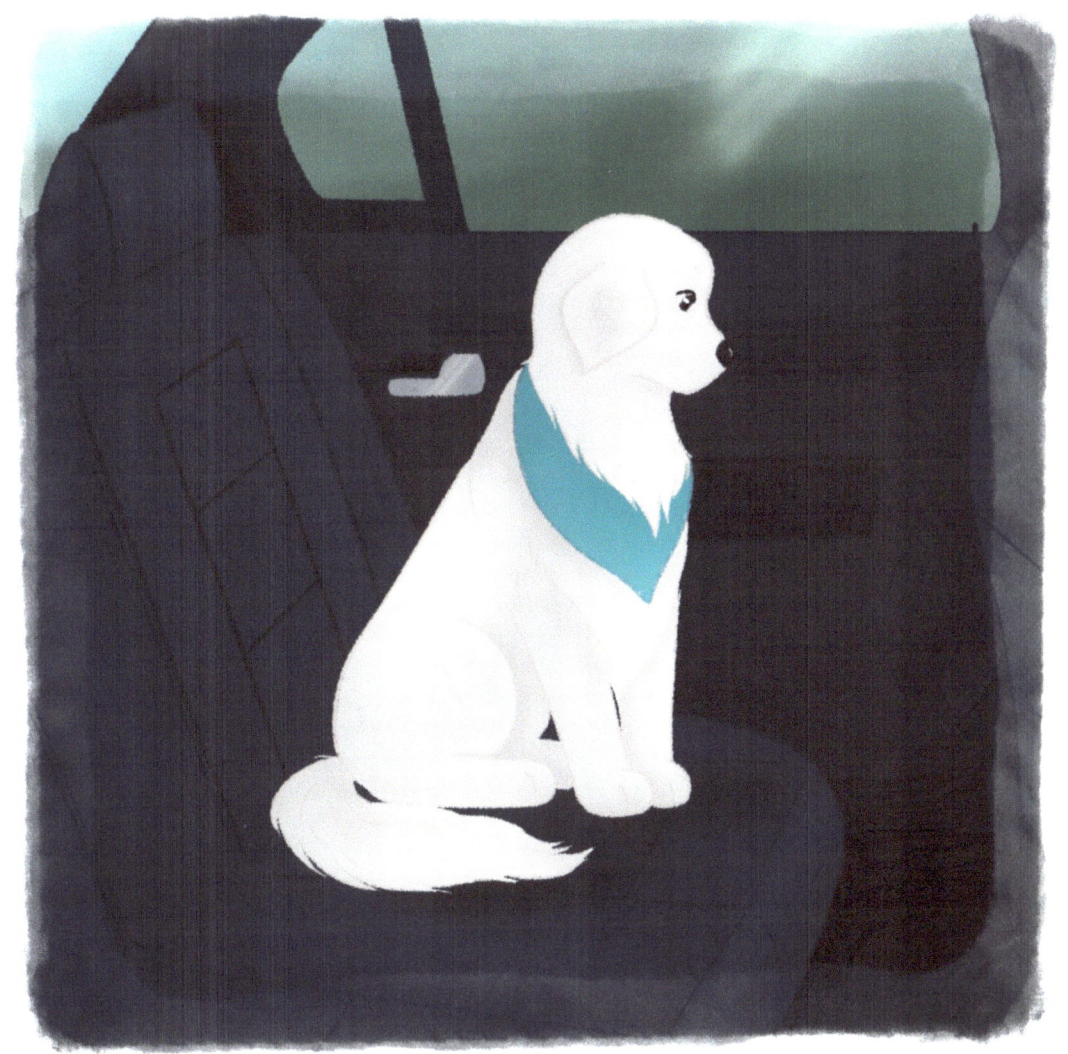

Maverick sat thinking about what Nash had said. "Then what can we do to make them happy?"

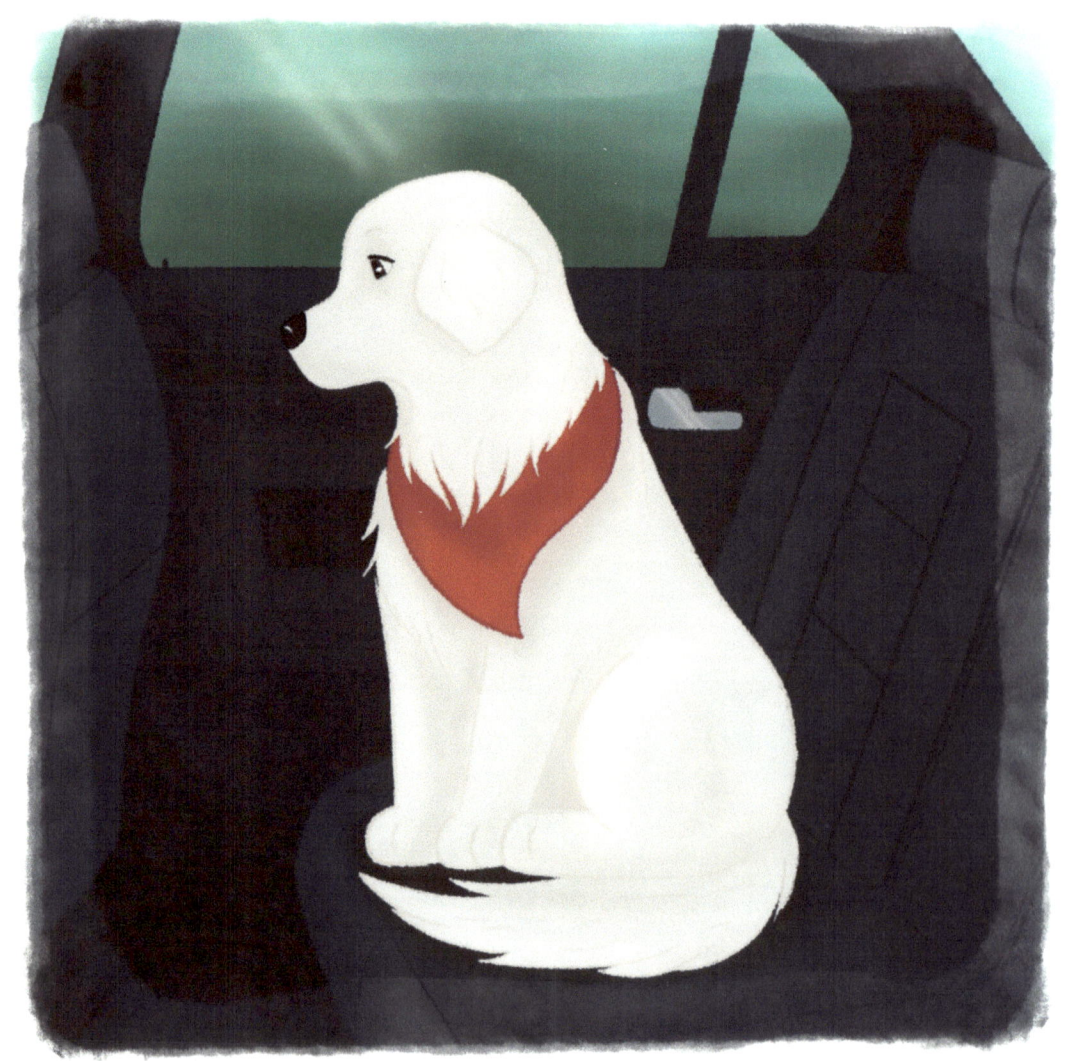

"Well, if it's okay with the patient, we can walk into the room and give them lots of snuggles and love." Nash explained. Maverick then nodded.

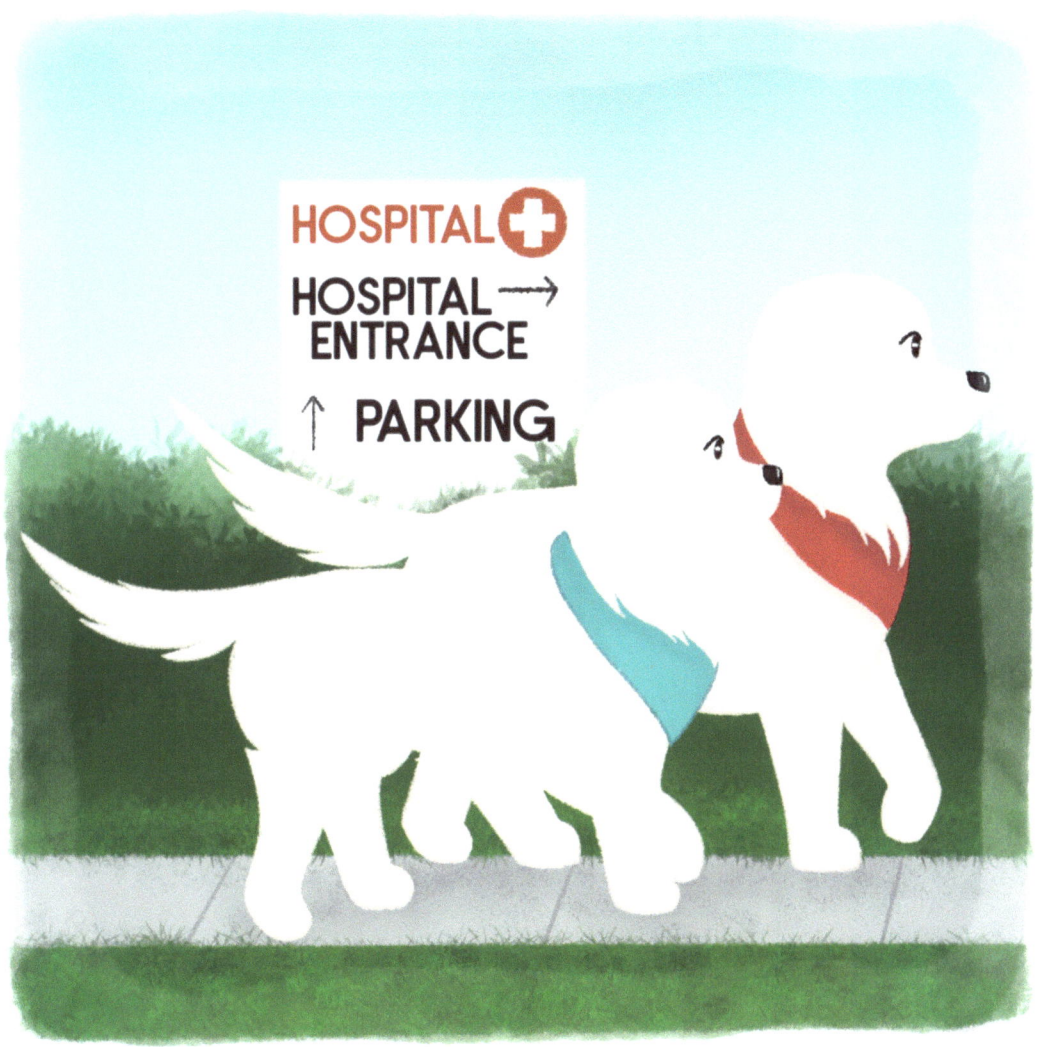

When they arrived at the hospital, Maverick followed closely behind Nash.

Once they reached the front desk, Maverick and Nash waited patiently as the humans talked to each other.

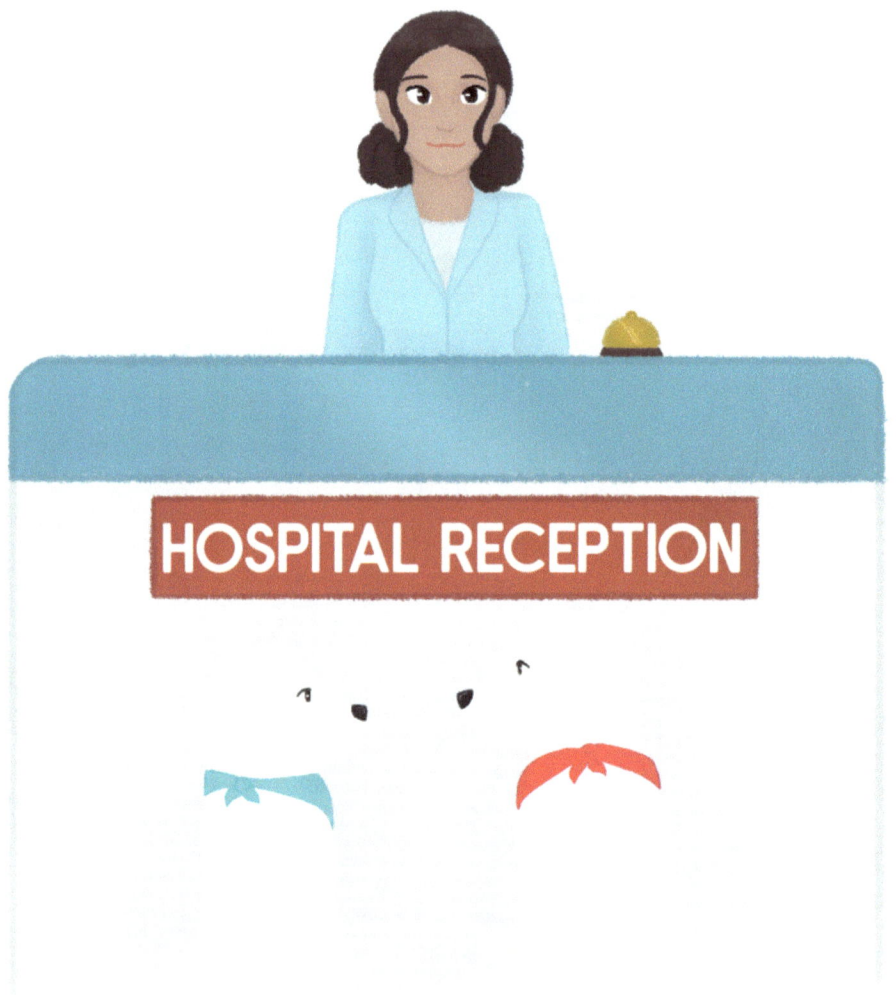

Then the nurse led them down a long hallway with rooms on either side.

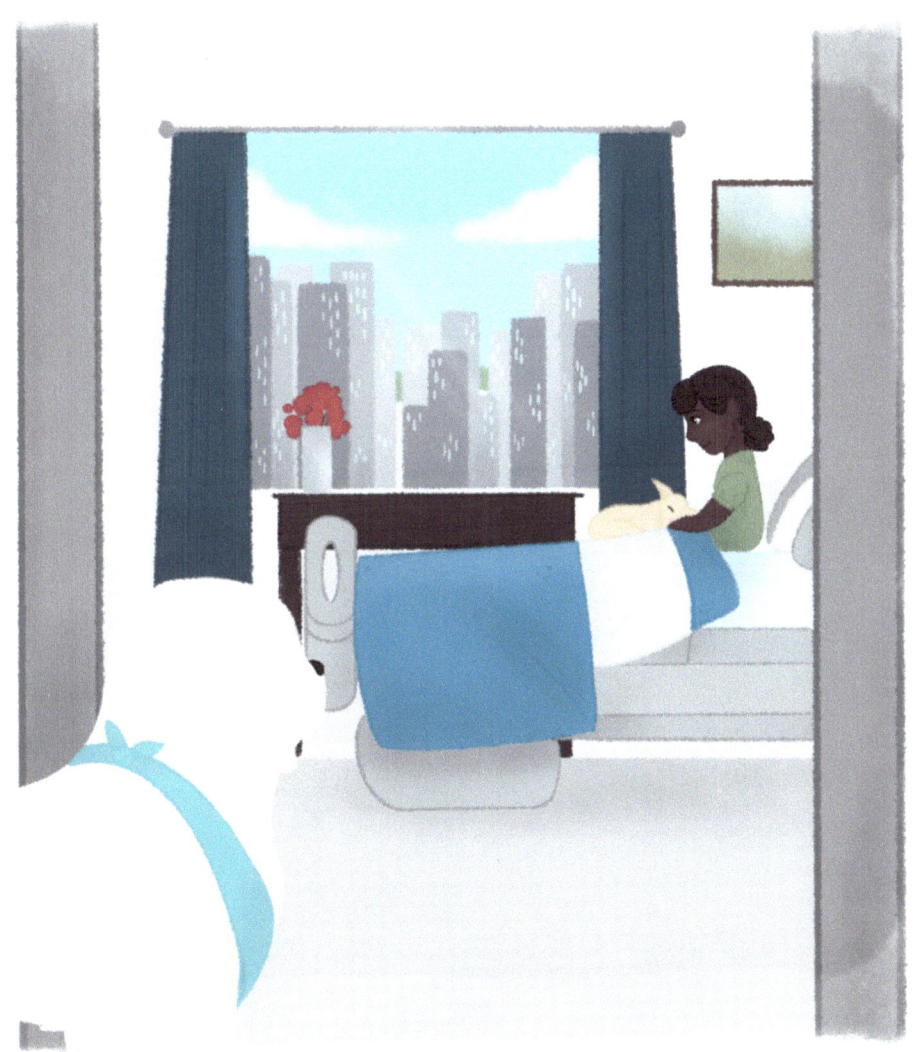

As Maverick walked passed open doorways, he peeked in to see other dogs cuddling and playing with different patients. Both young and old.

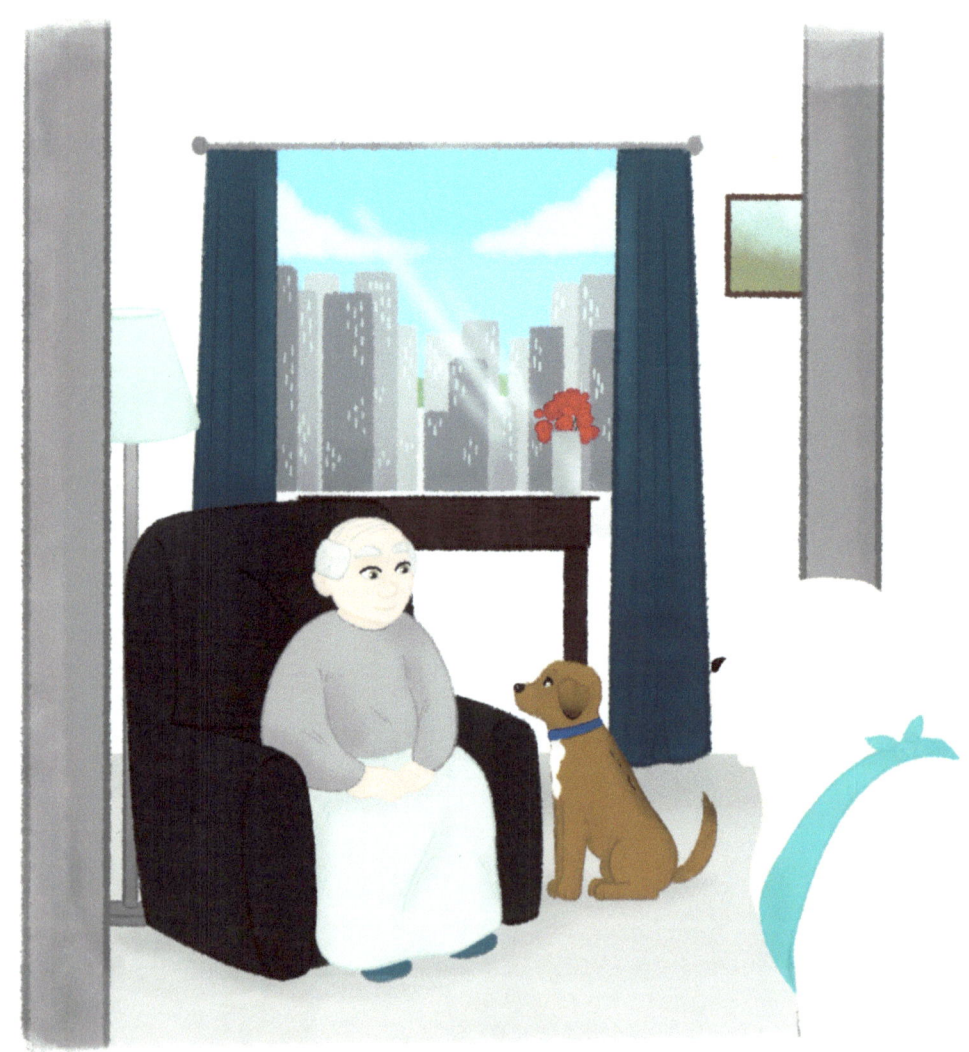

Maverick smiled to himself as he saw the joy on the patient's faces.

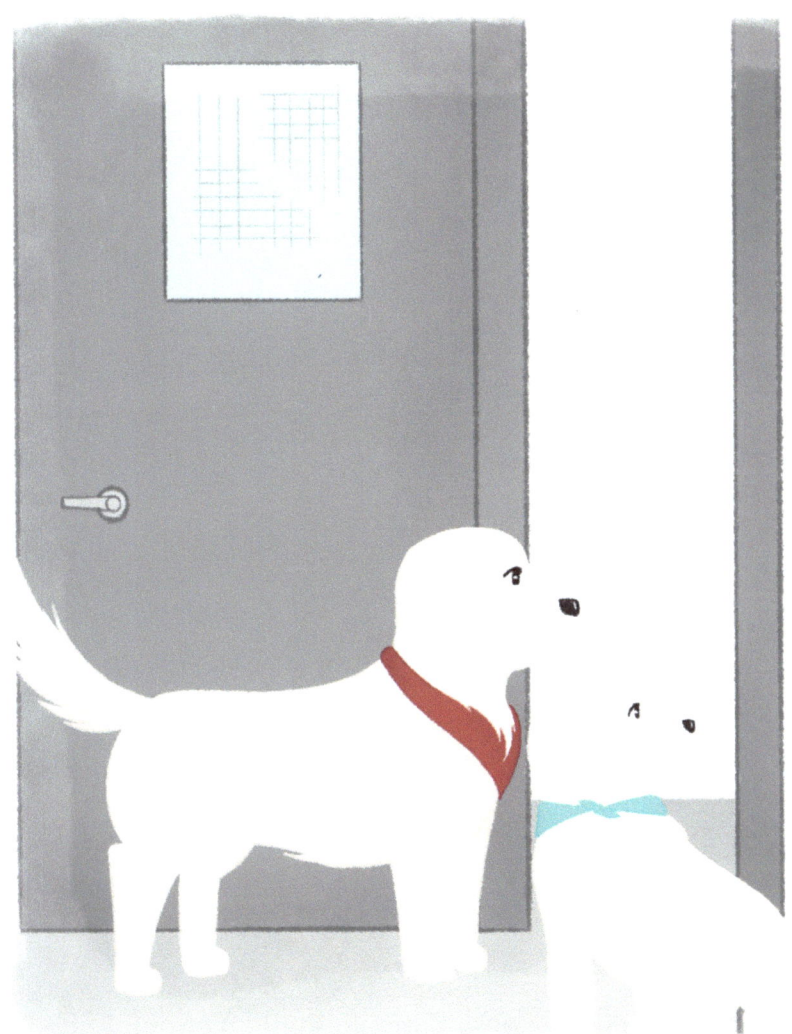

Finally, Maverick and Nash arrived at an open door at the end of the hall. Maverick then carefully peered into the room.

There sat a little boy in blue pjs. He was drinking some milk and eating a yummy looking sandwhich.

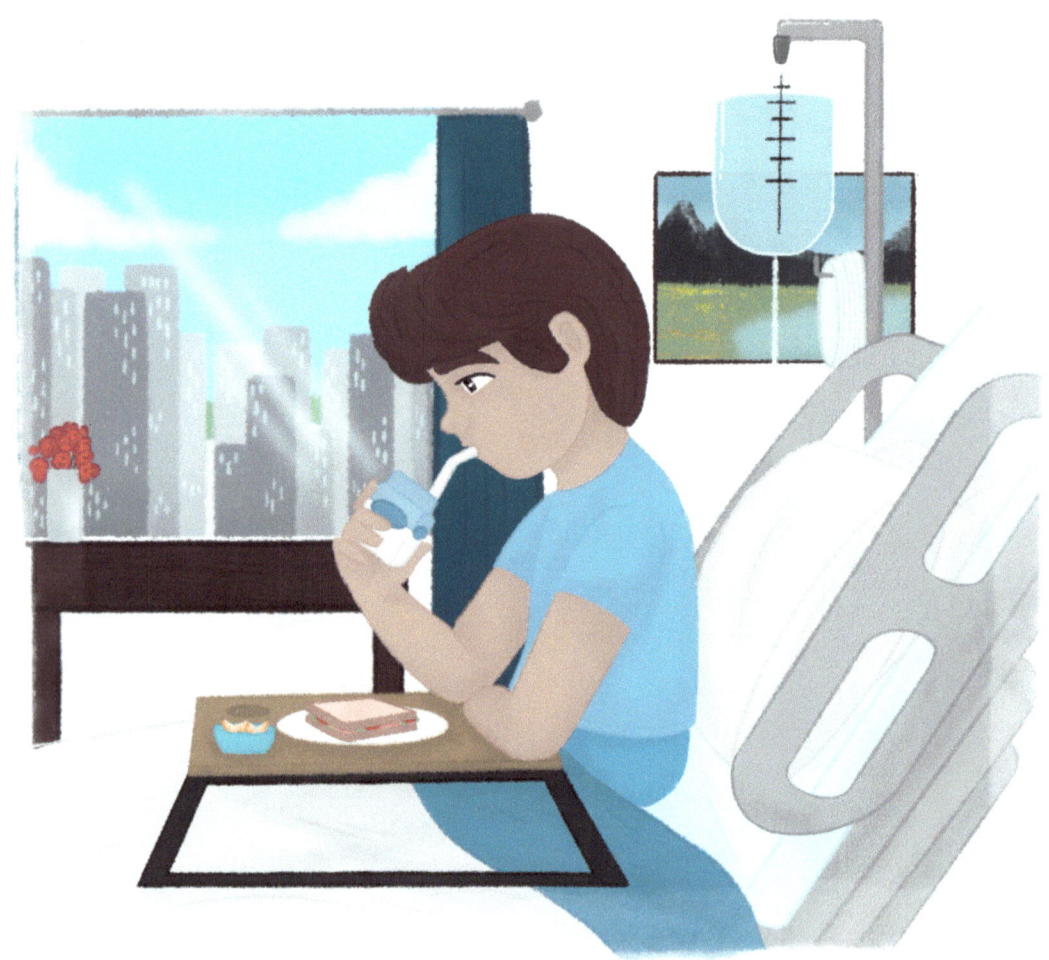

But as the little boy ate his lunch, Maverick couldn't find a hint of a smile on the boy's face.

The nurse that led Maverick and Nash to the patient's room, walked past them to the boy's bed.

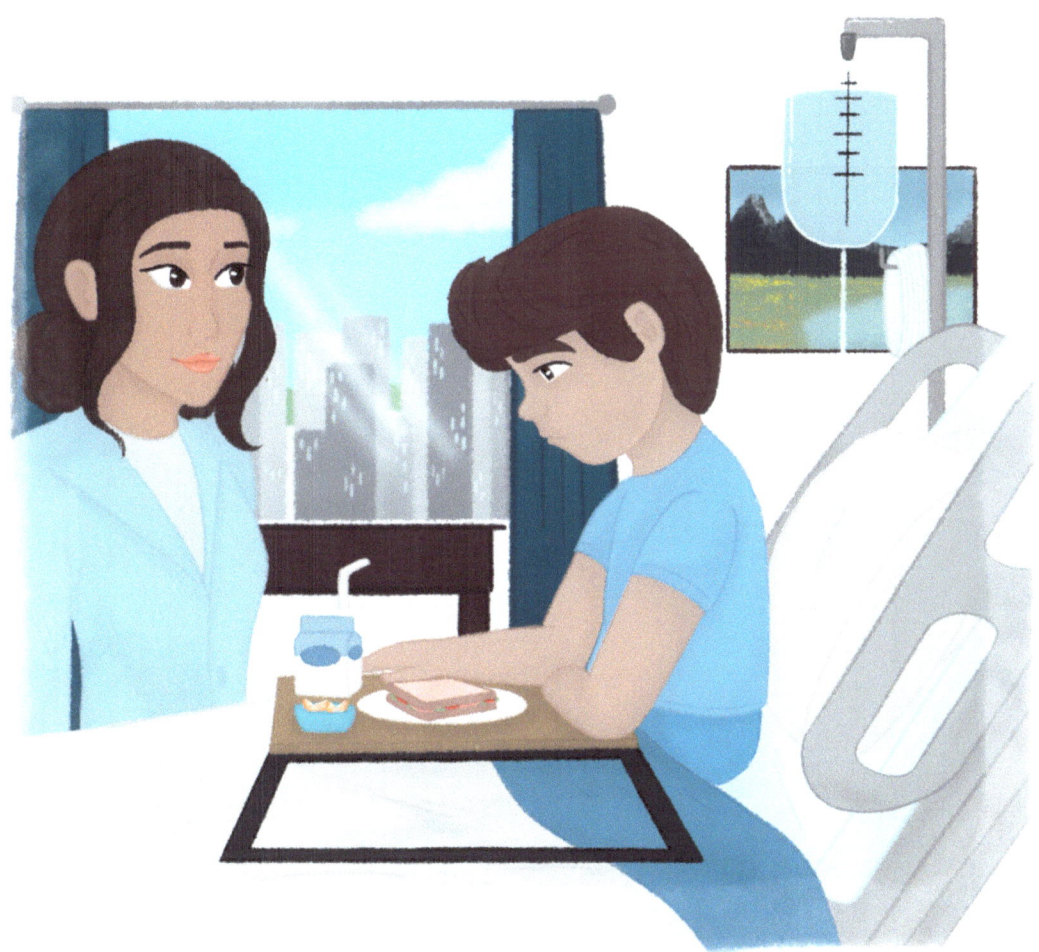

"Hello Logan!" The nurse said with a smile.
"How are you feeling?"

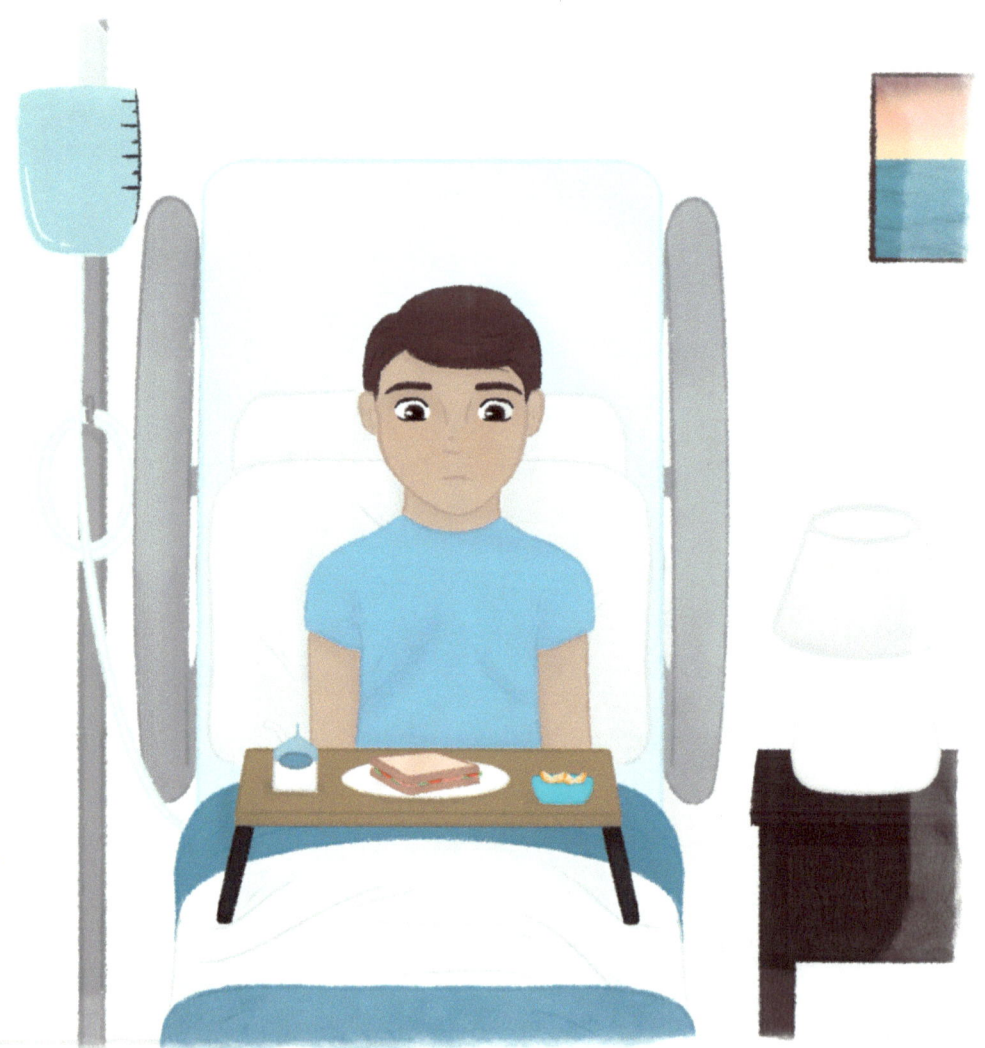

"Better, I guess." Logan shrugged.
"Well, how would you feel if I told you that I brought you a few visitors?" The kind nurse asked Logan with a smile.

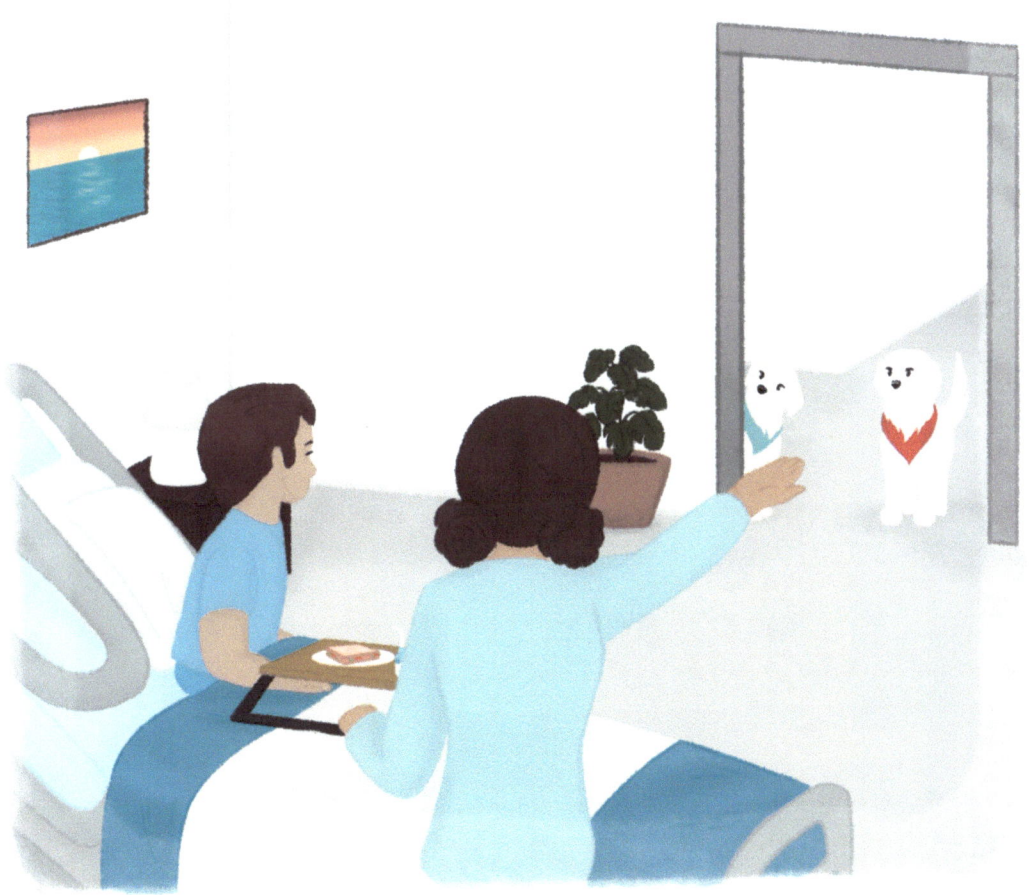

"Visitors, nurse Maria?" Logan asked with a quizzical brow. Nurse Maria nodded, then motioned for Maverick to come closer.

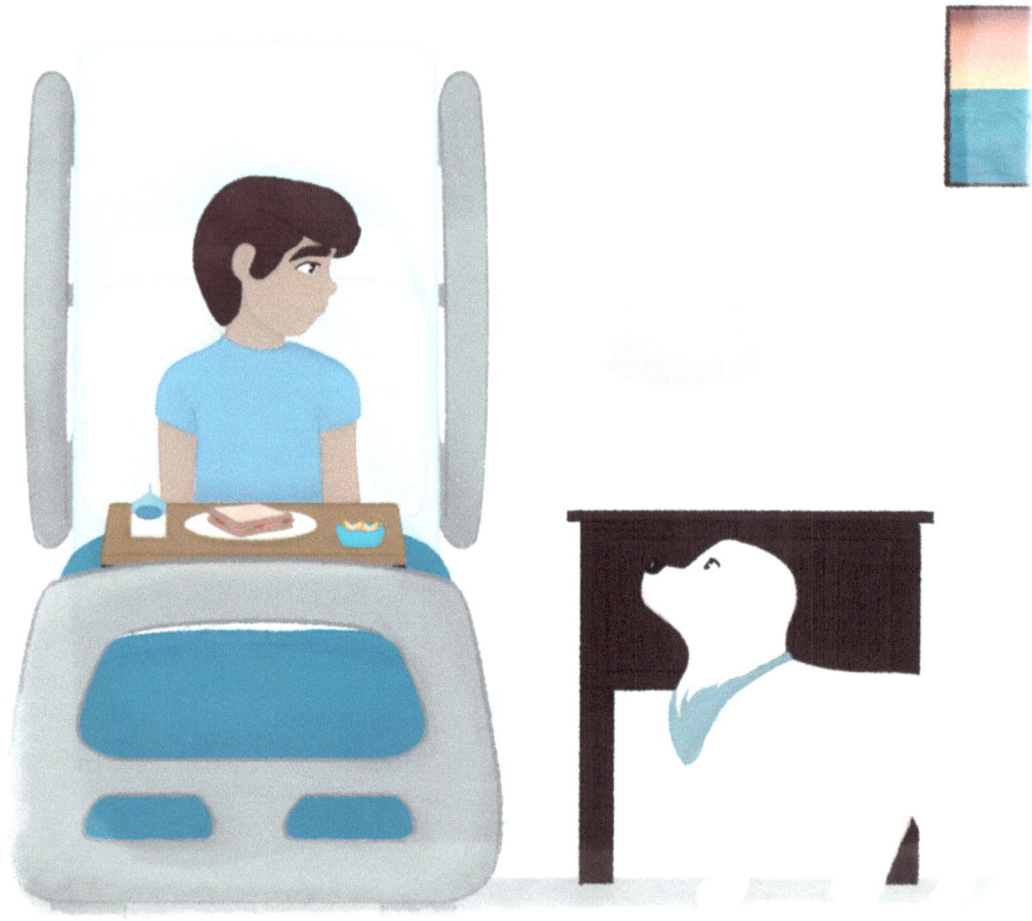

As Maverick tip toed in, he saw a smile creep on to Logan's face. "Doggies!" Logan exclaimed.

Maverick smiled as he put his two front paws on the little boy's bed.

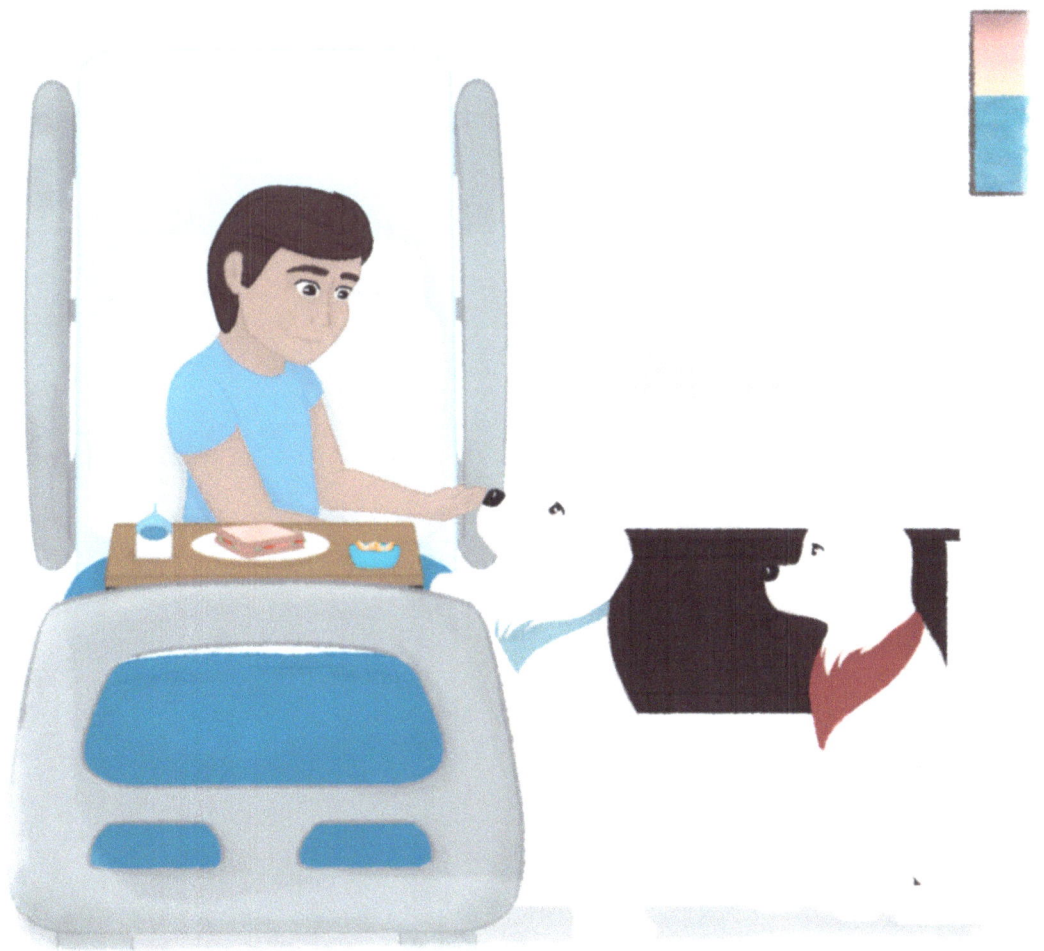

Logan then reached out to pet Maverick's head. "You're very soft." Logan stated with a joyful grin. "What are their names, nurse Maria?"

"Their names are Maverick and Nash!"
Nurse Maria answered.

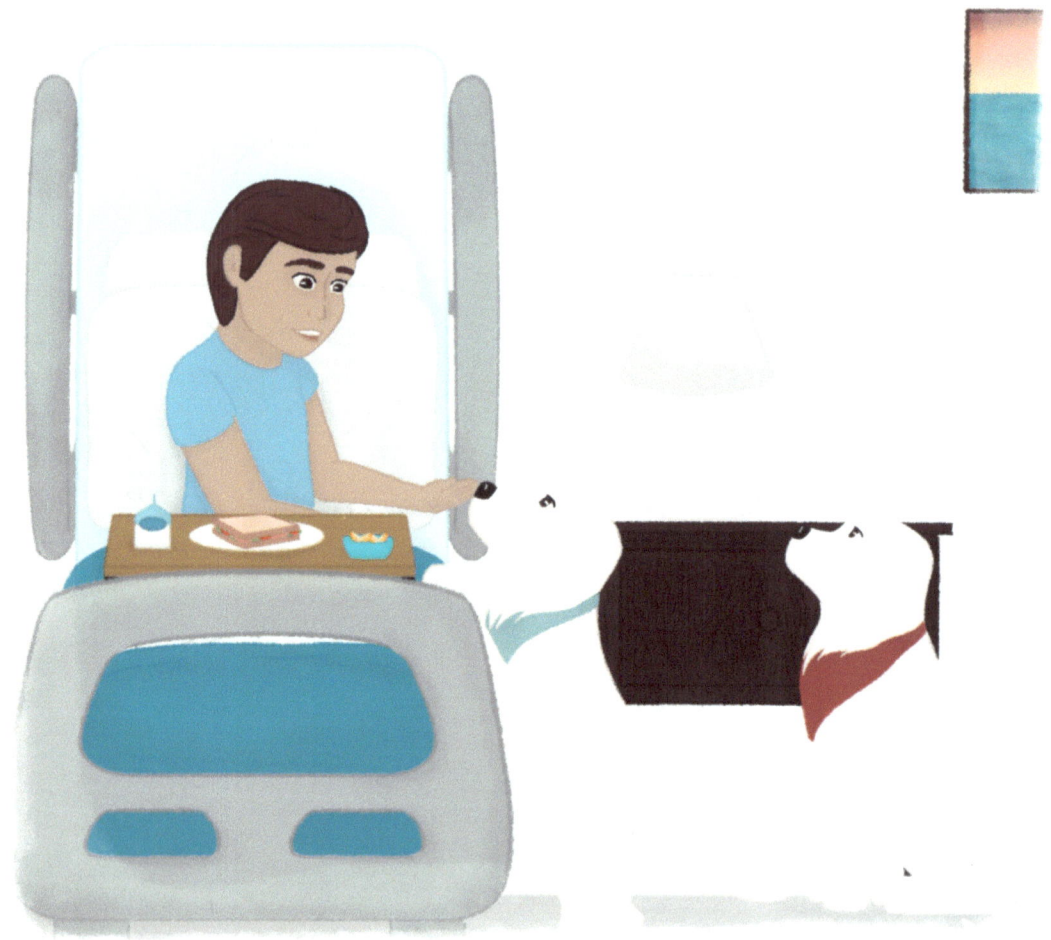

"Maverick and Nash." Logan whispered. "I like those names!"

Maverick was so happy to see Logan smiling.

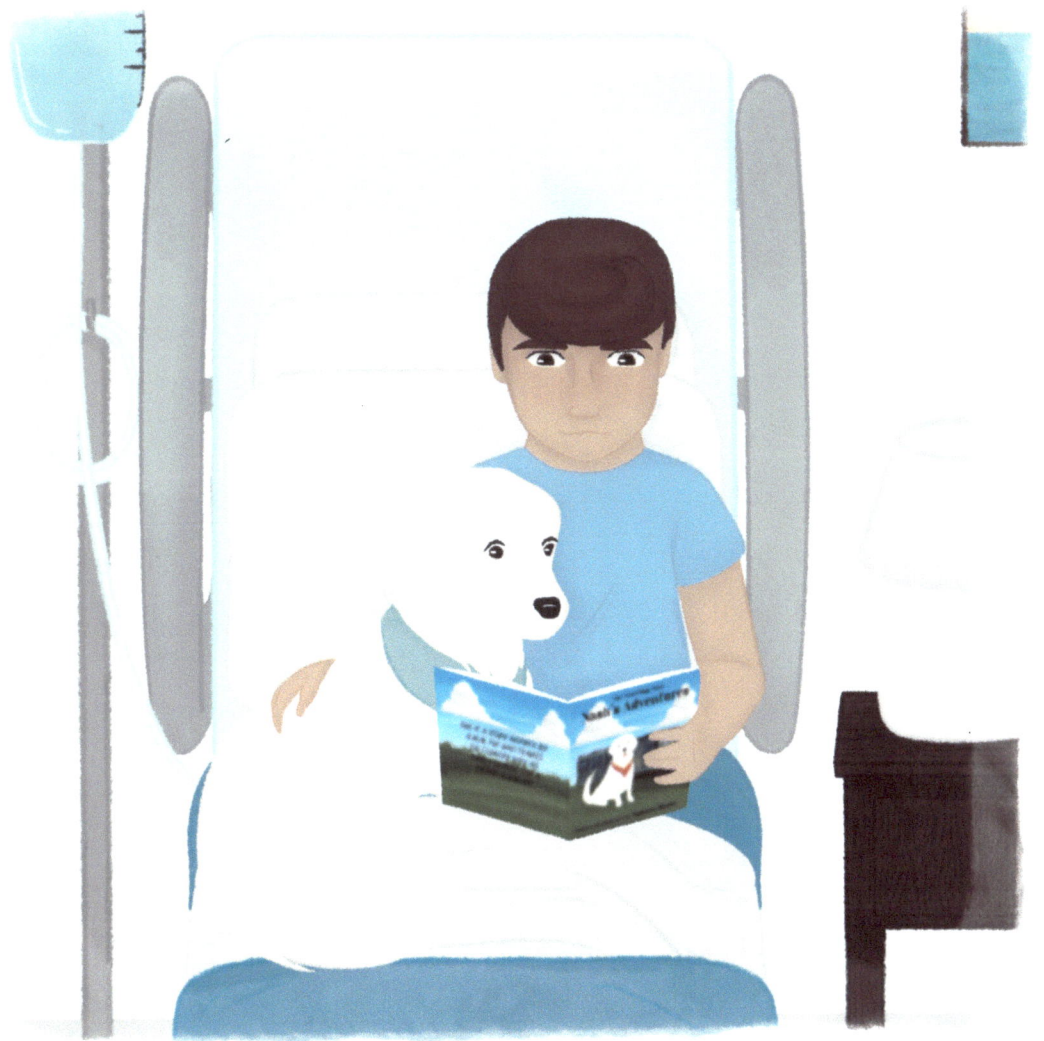

Maverick spent the rest of the day with Logan, snuggling and reading wonderful stories.

When it was time to go, Logan gave Maverick a big hug. "Thank you for visiting me, Maverick!"

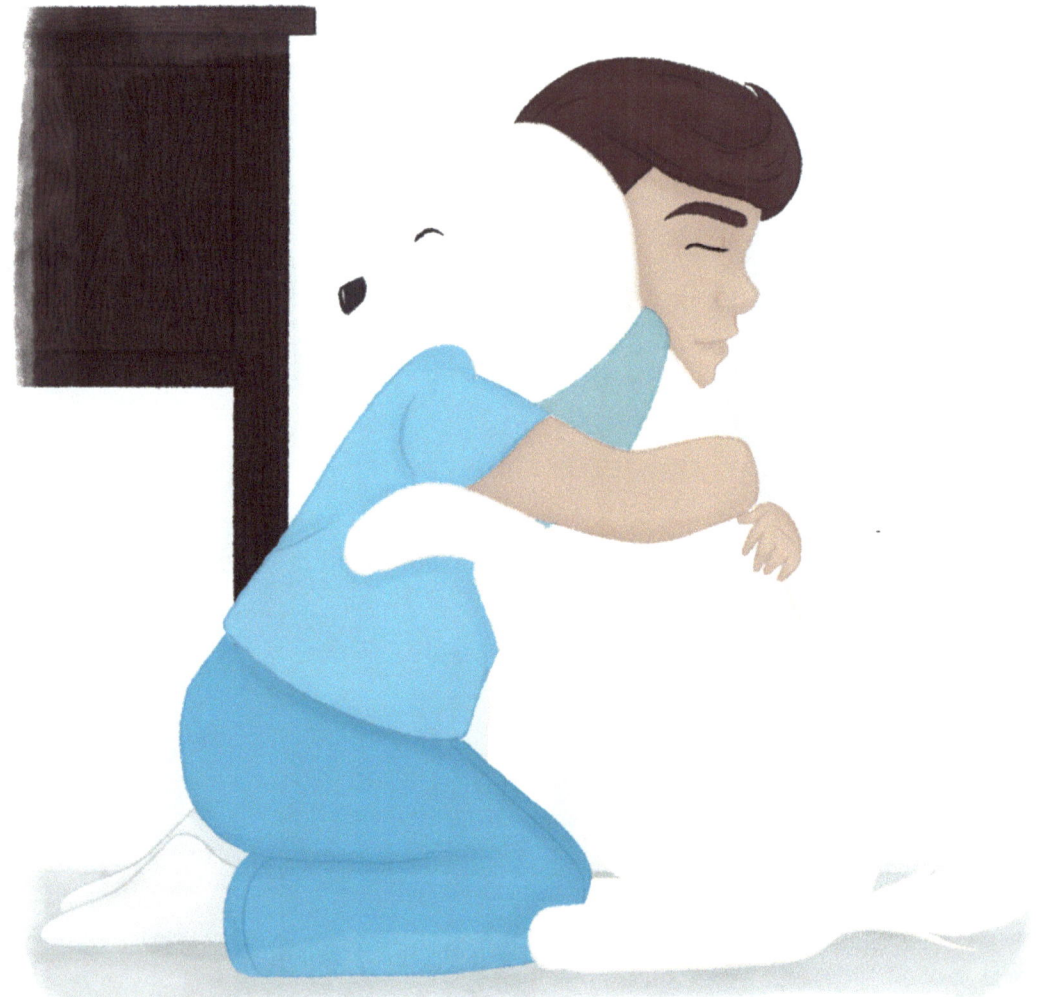

Maverick smiled on the inside. He was happy he met Logan and was able to make him smile.

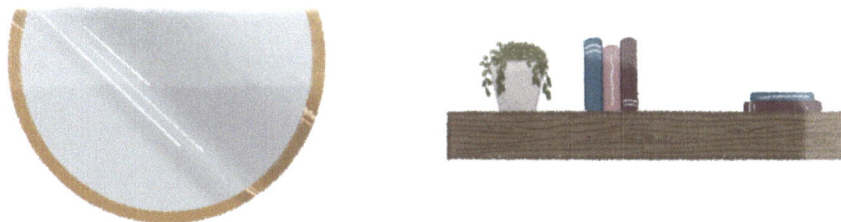
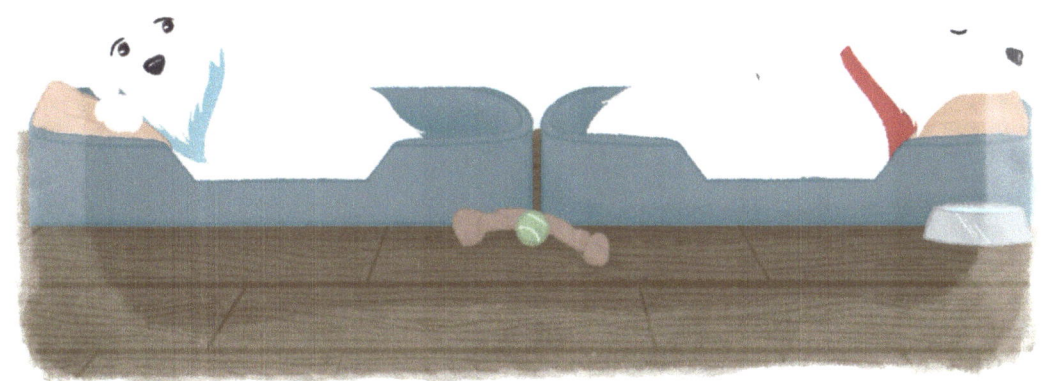

Later that night, Maverick curled up in his bed. As he laid down, a question formed in his head.

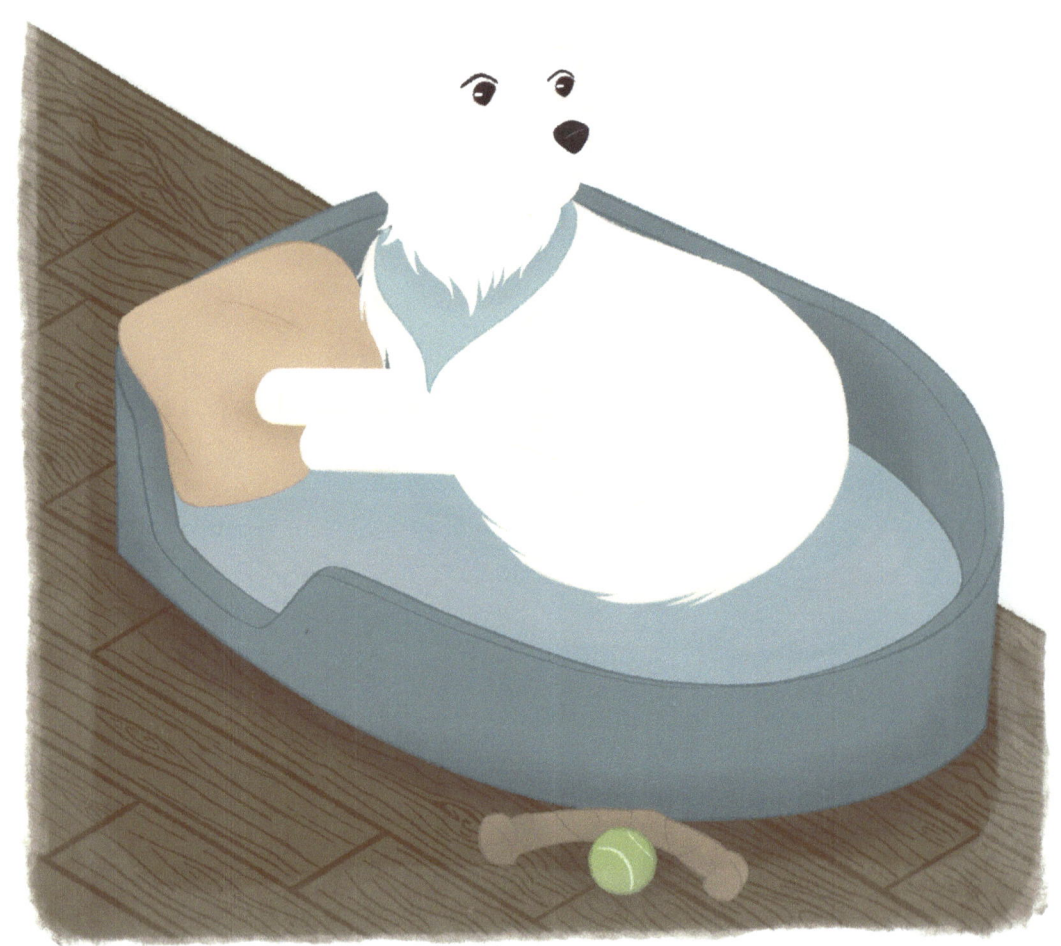

"Nash, you said it's the right thing to do when we serve others. But how do you know it's the right thing to do?" Maverick questioned.

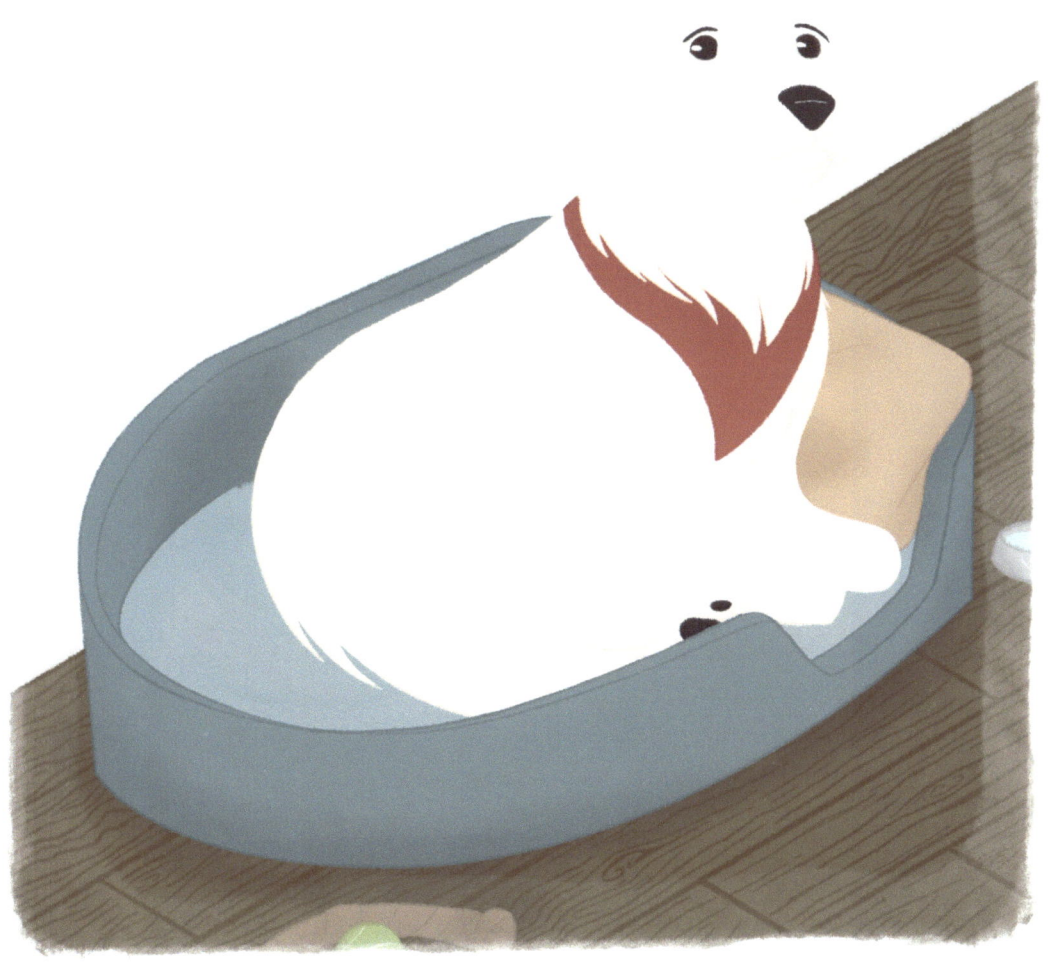

Nash gave a knowing smile. "Well, remember how I told you about Jesus? The man who was the Son of God who died on the cross for everyone's sins?"

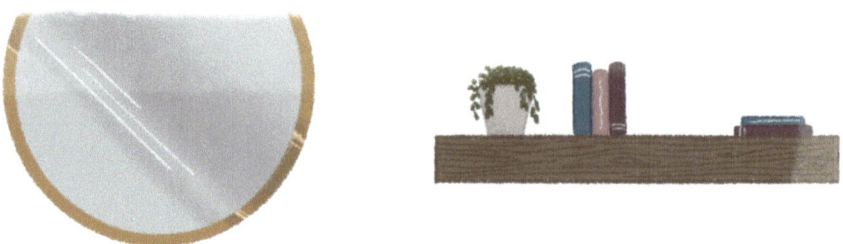
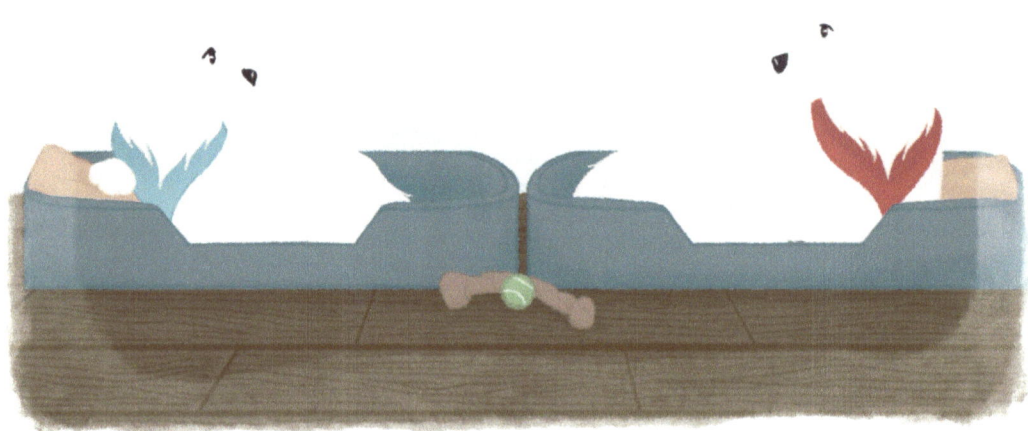

"Yes I do. That was very sad, but I'm happy He rose from the dead." Maverick said.

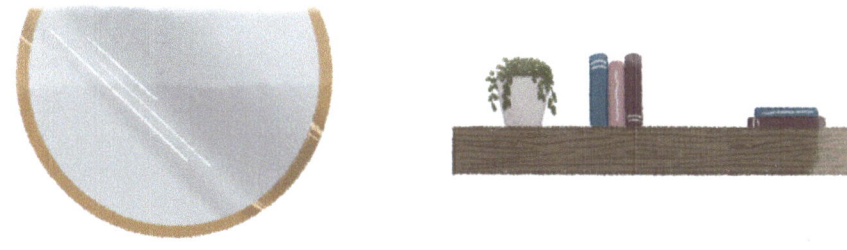

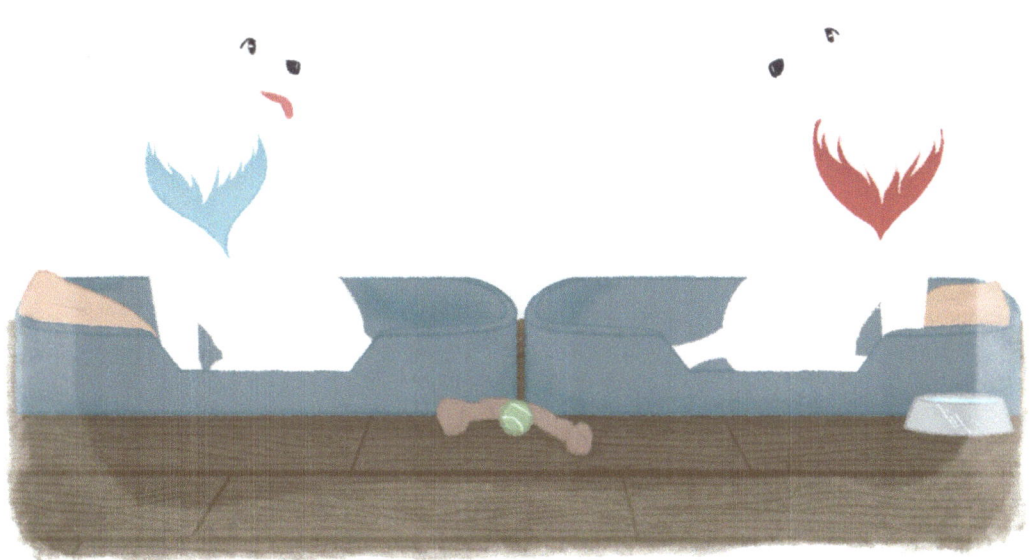

"Yes, me too. Well, Jesus told His followers that He came to serve and not be served. And we are to act like Jesus and serve others how He would." Nash explained kindly.

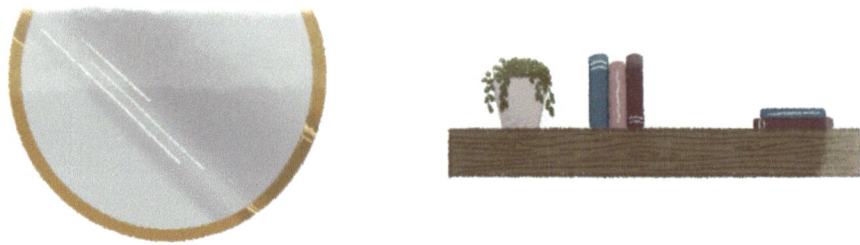
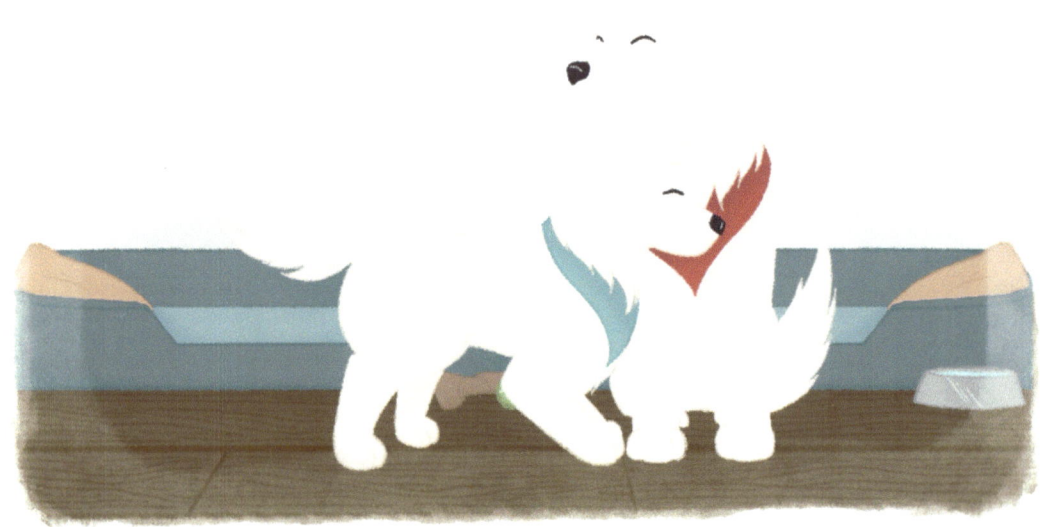

"Oh, that makes sense! Thank you big brother for showing me how to serve today!" Maverick exclaimed.
"You're welcome little brother." Nash said with a smile.

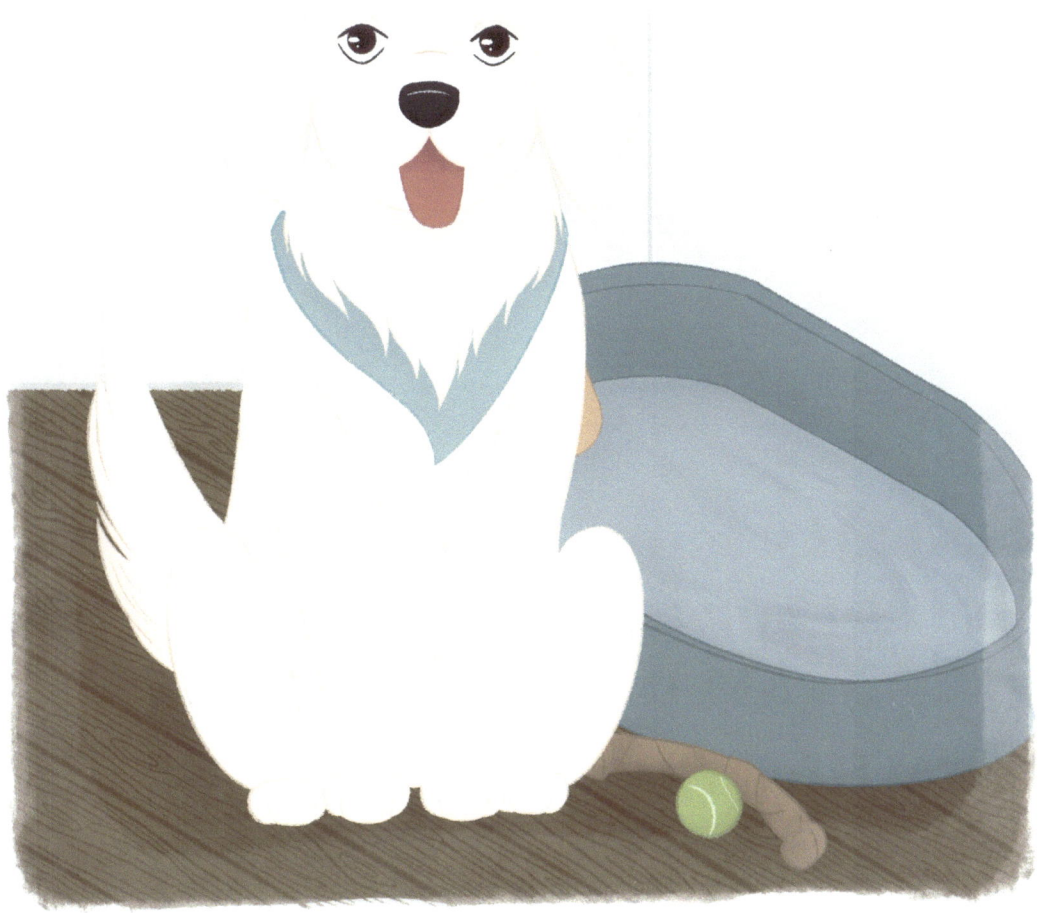

Maverick wagged his tail as he asked Nash, "When are we going to serve others next?"

The Author & Characters

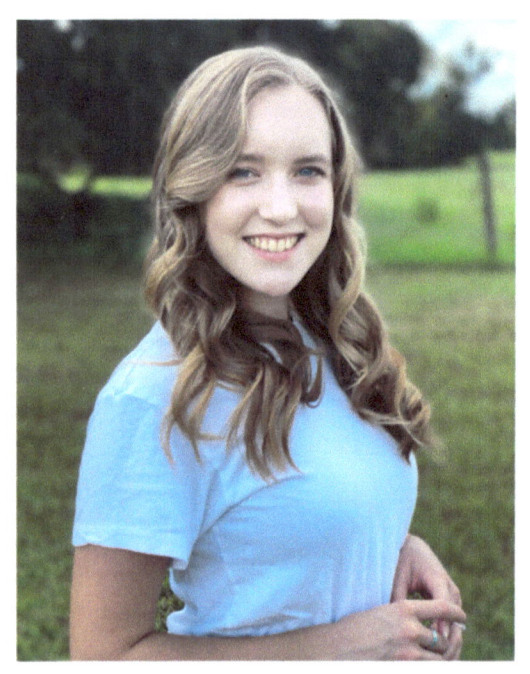 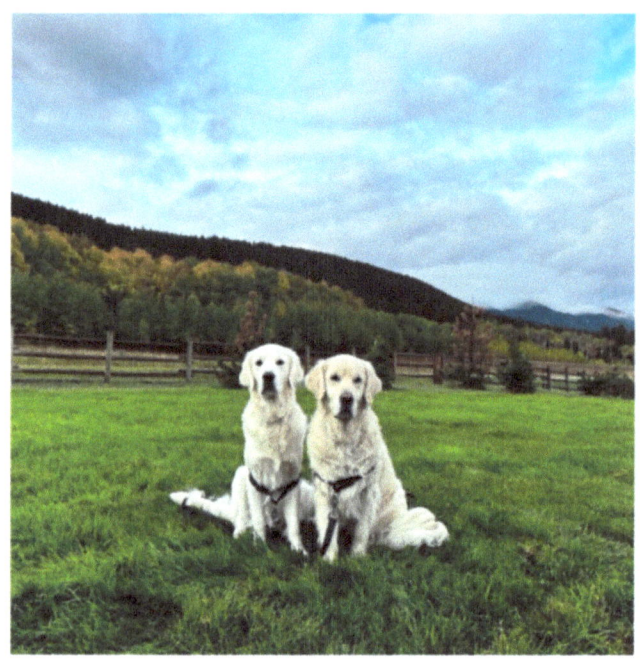

Hello! My name is Summer and I'm the author and illustrator of The Traveling Pack series!

The real life Maverick and Nash (shown above) are English Cream Retrievers who love to travel. You can find them at @pawsforlove on Instagram!

www.ingramcontent.com/pod-product-compliance
Lightning Source LLC
Chambersburg PA
CBHW051819210526
45473CB00005B/1660